Unlocking Your Better Days
Moving Forward After Adversity

Leonard Chatman, Jr.

ROYSTON Publishing

BK Royston Publishing
P. O. Box 4321
Jeffersonville, IN 47131
502-802-5385
http://www.bkroystonpublishing.com
bkroystonpublishing@gmail.com

© Copyright – 2018

All Rights Reserved. No part of this book may be reproduced, stored in a retrieval system, or transmitted by any means without the written permission of the author.

Cover Design: Jeremie Roberts

ISBN-13: 978-1-946111-56-2

Printed in the United States of America

Acknowledgements

First And Foremost

I thank my Lord and Savior Jesus Christ for giving me wisdom to complete this project. I'm grateful of the Holy Spirit for guiding me to express the things that will ultimately Unlock Better Days for all readers.

I'm extremely thankful for my great-grandparents who instilled the morals and values that has made me the man I am today.

To my mom who is an absolute beautiful soul and been my rock throughout my life. I thank you for the nuggets you have given me over the years and I will never forget them. Thank you for your resolute character. You bring so much sunshine to the lives of others and I am proud to be your son.

To my granny "Dotty", I could never verbally express how thankful I am for you. Since November of 1999 you have been the matriarch of our family and I appreciate our talks, our ice cream dates and most of all your collard greens.

To my mentors over the years: Wesley T. Leonard, Charlie McClendon, Lionel Campbell, Don Johnson and Terence Byrd. THANK YOU!!!

To my closest friends: Dan Dugger, Roderick "MO" Morris, Sedrick Childress, Mike Coplin, Emmanuel Rupert, Victor "Tory" Crumity and Shaune Mckinnie. Each of you have played a critical role in my life and I appreciate our laughs and friendship. I will never be able to successfully articulate the value you have added to my life so please accept my "Thank you."

To my mother in love: Thank you for everything and know without any doubt I love you dearly.

To my beautiful wife Monique, thank you from the bottom of my heart for pushing me to complete this book even when I was ready to give up. You are my absolute everything and I love you beyond words.

To my wonderful children to whom have not entered this world yet. By the time you are able to read this book, thousands if not millions of people will have read this, but always remember I had you in mind when writing this to leave a lasting legacy for our family and something you will be able to look back on. I love you!

Table of Contents

Acknowledgements	iii
Foreword	ix
Introduction	xi
Chapter 1 Where Does it Hurt?	1
Chapter 2 Forward March	19
Chapter 3 What's Your Equation?	35
Chapter 4 Managing Your Moments	51
Chapter 5 Divine Isolation	65
Chapter 6 Responsibility and Ownership	81
Chapter 7 Immunity From interruptions	93

Foreword

From the first moment I saw the title of this book "Unlocking Your Better Days" I knew this would be an asset to the reader from any aspect of life. The Young, the Old, the Rich, the Poor. No matter your back ground. In today's world barely a day, hour, minute or second goes without you hearing about someone needing assistance because they have been hurting not externally, but internally.

A glance through the pages of this book will show that there are better days ahead for the reader. This book consists largely of practical strategies and wisdom on facing hurt and moving forward. This book provides a valuable window on information assurance and covers the necessary components when it comes to unlocking better days.

    Don Johnson

Introduction

At any given time in life, there will be moments where hurt and pain will become an all too familiar visitor. The inevitability of pain should never be surprising nor should it be a constant in your life. I hear your voice even as you read, in that sometimes things are easier said than done. I get it! You've been hurt, you've been wounded, you've been scared and you've been scandalized, but did you read the title of this book? It's time we find the keys to unlock our better days. My hope is that you embrace this book with a spirit of understanding that the answers and solutions to walking in some of the best days of your life are a matter of YOU. When life comes knocking at the footsteps on your journey, we all need a reminder that we can make it through and move forward after adversity. I vividly recall a mentor who was instrumental during a particular season of my life. I was in Orlando, Florida, and Wesley T. Leonard said, "If you keep saying good morning, life and trouble will introduce itself to you." I didn't understand the magnitude of his statement until trouble really began to be an unwelcomed visitor on my journey to fulfilling the assignment and purpose God had designed for me. It's amazing how God will place the right people in your life at the right time. Their specific purpose is so HE can orchestrate His intended results through you. Can you imagine how awesome that is to know that someone is always in your corner consistently maneuvering things and people to produce the best version of YOU? Today is the best day of your life. You made a conscious decision to move forward, despite what was thrown at you, (and for some many) regardless of the opposition, (and for some plenty); nonetheless today is Moving Forward Day! As I was writing this book, it brought back many fond memories and painful moments that reminded me of the scripture in 2 Corinthians 12:9. It reads, "My grace is sufficient for thee: for my strength is made perfect in weakness. Most gladly, therefore, will I rather glory in my infirmities, that the power of Christ may rest upon me." I love that passage from the Apostle Paul because he demonstrated to us on numerous occasions, staggered through God's word, that trouble will make its approach in the most informal and intrusive way. But God's grace is just the dosage of inspiration I need to make it. I sincerely hope you enjoy reading this book. I intend for it to motivate, inspire, and move you to another level of faith and beyond your known comfort zone. This book is a series of #FiresideChats and experiences throughout my journey. I believe it will serve as your springboard not only to move you forward when life seems to keep taking you backwards, but to stay moving forward. To get the most out of this book, I recommend having intimate prayer time before and after reading. This will set the atmosphere to move you closer to freedom, independence, self-awareness, and determination so whatever the enemy delivers, God's power will propel you to deliverance. I urge you to consider committing yourself to each chapter, no matter what happens and things will happen NEVER QUIT. My hope is that you will find something from within to move forward after adversity because life is worth living.

Chapter 1

Where Does it Hurt?

On Christmas day, do you remember receiving a new bike and being so excited to go outside and finally ride without any training wheels? You got on the bike only to fall to the ground in utter pain emotionally and physically. Maybe you are not able to relate to the bicycle analogy, but I'm certain putting your hand on the hot stove and getting burned suits your recollection better. Either scenario, whether failing to the ground in pain with scrapped knees and the infamous "strawberry," or hand blisters from a burn, it was easy for you and your parent to locate the pain because you were forthcoming in letting them know where it hurts. I believe that's how life functions as well. When we fall it will hurt. When our loved ones unexpectedly pass away, the pain deepens. When you get married only to divorce two years later, the pain feels insurmountable. However, if you are to move forward after adversity and to experience better days, you have to come to a place where you are able to locate the pain and let your Father in heaven know what is ailing you. Locating the pain is one-step closer to healing and while the pain will not be mitigated, it will send a signal to the enemy that Isaiah 54:17 conveyed. "No weapon formed against you shall prosper." I remember getting a bicycle for Christmas one year, and inevitably falling and meeting face to face with skin and concrete because I thought I was strong and capable enough to handle this new experience of riding without the training wheels. Nonetheless, my mother was instantly made aware of my pain because of my tears, elevated voice, and the blood-stained pants. Just like any other mother would have done, she came to the rescue and asked a litany of questions from;

- What Happened?
- Who were you with?
- Where does it hurt?

The last question is always the most critical on the journey to healing. If you are not able to pinpoint or locate the pain, how can you possibly begin the process of healing? Or better yet, if you ignore what is actually causing the pain, and choose to do nothing about it, how can you possibly position yourself towards healing? Before you read another line or chapter of this book, for it to benefit you the most, let's have an affirmation activity exercise.

Affirmation Activity - Repeat multiple times until you feel there is a sense of preparation in your soul.

"I will acknowledge what has caused my pain."

"I will address what has caused my pain."

"I will adjust as needed."

Now that we have affirmed our stance on locating our pain, you can move closer to healing. Oftentimes, the misconception regarding healing and walking through the process is because you have made a decision to heal that the damage never existed, and today we dispel that notion! Making the decision to locate your pain, acknowledge it, address it, and adjust it means that whatever the determining factor was for the cause of your pain, no longer controls you. When something, or in some cases someone, no longer controls you it no longer has any power; therefore it's time to move forward. By no means am I attempting to minimize your struggle or your pain, but what am I suggesting are several things that you can incorporate in your life as valued principles from my series of #FiresideChats.

A) Healing can only begin when you shift your focus from **Pain to the Power of God's Voice**.

B) Healing can only begin when you shift your attention from the **Debilitation of Pain** to the **Demonstration of God's Power.**

C) Healing can only begin when our understanding is that **Pain causes Dislocation**, but **God's Power has Relocation**

D) **God's Reputation will meet you in any Location**

When you dislocate a bone in your body, it essentially disturbs the normal arrangement or position of something and that is ultimately the example of our lives. The pain has disrupted and disturbed our only sense of normalcy, and we have to pick up the pieces. Although dislocation is uncomfortable, God's power will relocate your heart and mind to a space of strength and fortitude. Would you like to hear some GREAT NEWS? Although you may face difficult challenges, knowing that God will face them with you is tremendous news. You must remember what Jesus said in Matthew 28:20, "I am with you always, even until the end of the world." That is the epitome of God's reputation. He is constant, unshakeable, unconquerable, and unmovable. God's reputation is all throughout His word and when you feel the walls are caving in, always open the Bible to remind you of the things that HE has promised.

- I the Lord will go down before you and will be with you. (Deuteronomy 31:8)
- I will not leave you, nor forsake you. (Hebrews 13:5)
- I am a refuge for the oppressed, and a stronghold in times of trouble. (Psalm 9:9)
- He heals the brokenhearted and binds up their wounds. (Psalm 147:3)
- Weeping has an expiration date of only a night because you will experience joy in the morning. (Psalm 30:5)

Admittedly, the pain we experience from challenges are inevitable and inconceivable. When you make the decision to move forward in spite of that pain, you are directly letting the enemy know your strength and resolve has more power than his attacks. Pain is not predictable, but it should not paralyze you to the extent that you cannot move forward. Taking on the concept to move forward after adversity, results in unlocking better days for you. It requires a certain level of growth, but more importantly a certain attitude, to which we will discuss in the next chapter. I'm sure you remember the phrase, "No Pain, No Gain" and more than likely heard it in various forms whether you were exercising, or trying to accomplish a personal goal. This phrase has been embedded in the minds of everyone. Truthfully, as life progresses and experiences seem to come frequently, it has so much validity and character to it.

- You can only grow through the threshold of pain. While it may be uncomfortable temporarily. Don't run from what was designed to develop you not destroy you. #FiresideChat

The pain I've experienced over the course of my life from failed relationships, employment fiascos, and financial crisis all have helped me to understand the totality of pain. Pain maturates, pain increases awareness, and pain increases tolerance. Then when other circumstances arise, you will have the stamina to endure and the wherewithal to move forward after your adversity. I'm confident we all can remember times where we were completely tired, burned out, or simply exhausted and stamina was not even a thought or consideration. As awkward and unorthodox as it may sound, pain possesses the power to groom us for growth. It's true indeed, because society has conditioned our minds to think pain is lasting or pain is there to destroy, but in all actuality, it is the opposite. Let's have an honest moment: I do NOT welcome pain, but I also do not discourage it because soon one day you will look back over a period of time and say those words that the gospel singer Marvin Sapp famously said in his song, "Never Would Made it. I'm Stronger, I'm Wiser, I'm Better, Much Better."

Aren't you joyful that what was intended to throw you into a state of depression was not demoralizing? Aren't you thankful that while the pain was present and persistent it did not paralyze you? As you continue your journey, make constant reminders to yourself that you were not built to break, but you were built to build others via your own experiences. What's a better way to encourage and inspire others than through using your voice to tell what you did to become a survivor, and overcomer? Don't allow your pain to be funneled down a drain, or don't allow what you've experienced to be wasted all because you have chosen to be silent. My public speaking journey has been just that, a "journey." But how selfish it would be for me to hoard the ups and down I've encountered, versus sharing with another rising speaker to prevent them from dashing into the headaches I've met. I remember being interviewed by WJXT, a local news station in Jacksonville, Florida, and something came out of my mouth unrehearsed, unchoreographed to the extent I surprised myself, and that was "you have a voice and a choice."(That was good!) Today you have a choice to either hoard your story about life's challenges, or help someone else by sharing your story. Doing so will provide a sense of encouragement to people and let them know they can make it, they will get through this, they can move forward after adversity because on the other side of your pain is the sweet promises of God.

So often, I've witnessed people having the propensity to hide or have this overwhelming sensation of embarrassment relating to the challenges that sent them into a whirl of pain. For example, frustration, anxiety, depression, sadness, lowliness, pessimism, cynicism, and the list of negative emotions can go on for the remainder of this chapter. Here is the dilemma in all of this. We are giving too much time and attention to those emotions. If we are to unlock the best days of our lives, it's time we stop hiding what we've been through in life. To unlock your better days, and let's be clear, they are within reach and arm's length, you have to navigate successfully through a process I call the "Give Up" process. There are some things you must give up if you are to move forward after adversity. Give up habits, hurts, and hang-ups. Sometimes you have to give up people who are toxic to your maturation, toxic to your growth, toxic to your peace and toxic to your wellbeing. If you have people in your life like this, it's time you give them up. When you operate emotively it will be hard to completely drop or give up some of the things that are detrimental to you, but you have to come to a place that suggests, "I AM MORE IMPORTANT."

A Key to Unlocking your Better Days is properly aligning value to those things that will not place you in position to move forward. What does that mean? For example, if during this "give up" process you recognize there are some people you need to "give up," then you align your thoughts with this sentiment: "If their presence cannot add value to your life, then their absence will not make a difference." (Unknown Author of Quote)

Let me be clear, sometimes during this "giving up" phase, it will possibly place you in a position of embarrassment. However, you have to be so confident in your faith that you know assuredly that God is going to use your Embarrassment for the other person's Empowerment. #FiresideChat

God can and will use your situation to encourage somebody else; thus, the critical importance is to never be ashamed of what you are dealing with. God has supreme power to use your Testimony to Teach your neighbor, and that's where you can begin to see the locks being removed and your better days shining from heavenly sunlight. My encouragement to you is:

- Stop hiding your betrayals
- Stop hiding your divorce
- Stop hiding your molestation
- Stop hiding your alcoholism

There have been countless opportunities for me to bless my neighbor. Not monetarily, but imparting some of the challenges I've experienced and how I was able to overcome them and move forward even in the face of adversity. When I embraced the totality of that ideology, I begin to witness God's not only unlocking my better days but unleashing them as if He was waiting on me to MOVE.

Could that be the answer to most things God is definitely waiting on us to decide which is the direction we want to travel? Could it be that God is ready to unleash the miraculous, but can't do so until you make a decision to MOVE FORWARD? Not only am I going to move forward, but also I declare and decree WE MARCH FORWARD. As you march forward, always remember God's Power has enough force to provide the proper provisions for you to experience His promises. (That was good!)

Chapter 2

Forward March

Technology has advanced quite tremendously over the years whether it's the internet capability, electronic mail, and my favorite "Call Forwarding." Why my favorite? The functionality is what's most impressive and intriguing to me. Think about it, if you need to be contacted and not lose a sense of the day, your telephone number can be forwarded so that you will not miss any incoming calls. Have you ever moved to another city, state, or just a simple address change and had the need to forward your mail? Of course, most of us have and that's how I view our lives. For you to unlock the best days of your life and move forward after adversity, it's imperative you take inventory of some things.

Forwarding means to help advance or promote something or send on to a further destination. When you are forwarding, inevitably there is a process of redirecting to another receiver. Even as you are reading this book, the world is in some very difficult days where there is a complete disregard for humanity that oftentimes we see result in mass shootings. Possibly you find yourself expecting to have better years than you've experienced historically, only to find yourself in the same constant struggle and now **disappointment** is taking its toll. Maybe you found a new friend and felt optimistic that he or she was "the one" only to be

discouraged by the outcome. Could it be that you've been expecting a miracle prophesied in your life that was going to bring you into a space of unspeakable joy, a space of immeasurable favor, only to be **demoralized** by this thing we call life? I'm sure you've held on to anxieties far too long and you've allowed the negative to affect you in such a way that you constantly are replaying things in your mind.

Let me remind you of the title of this chapter "Forward March," meaning as God is unlocking the best days of your life, hopefully you are simultaneously redirecting everything that has kept you back from truly living. I cannot itemize what has held you back, that is your job. My job is to provide the keys for you to walk in your better days.

Today is REDIRECTING Day. Reflect on the things that have caused you tremendous pain, hurt, anxiety, sadness, frustration, exasperation, disappointment, derailment, vexation, anger, irritation, discontentment, and aggravation. Reflect very briefly and redirect those things to a destination where length and breadth are not comprehendible (Heaven), and its receiver is almighty with supreme power (God). It's FORWARDING TIME. God gives us through His Word permissible access to forward anything preventing us from fully being able to move forward after adversity.

- 1 Peter 5:7 "Cast all of your anxiety on him because he cares for you."
- Psalm 55:22 "Cast your burden upon the Lord and he will sustain you."

- Psalm 34:15 "The eyes of the Lord are on the righteous, and his ears are open to their cry."

As you have begun to forward things to a divine destination, and beginning to make it through the "Give Up" process, you should have a sense of vibrancy about who you are. You are fully charged to become all God intended for you to be. Where it becomes problematic for some is they are 100% charged, but their battery is dead. I recall having moved to a new city known for experiencing all four seasonal changes. Over a period of two months, my car sometimes would not start, but all the while this car battery was relatively new. During the summer and fall months, there were no mechanical issues. However, as soon as the season changed from fall to winter, time after time I would need the assistance of a neighbor to give me a jump. Once my frustration boiled to a maximum after I was late for work one morning and stranded at a local McDonald's. Then I knew it was beyond time to take my car to the local auto store for a free battery check. The associate tested the battery and came back with a result that blew me away. He said, "Sir, you are operating on a 100% charged battery, but it is still dead." For the life of me, I could not fathom exactly what that meant. Was he speaking to me in mechanic's lingo, or could this be a new wave of communication? Could it be that God was teaching me a lesson through the simplicity of a car battery? I will choose the latter. The take away is, as God transitions you through various seasons of your life, you too just like the car battery, will have to be changed, replaced, or reinvented. God was giving me subtle messages to change my battery, but because I made a refusal I had to experience the consequence. Never fight against WHAT God intends for your life, and never battle with God for WHO He intends for you to be.

"Sometimes who God wants you to be, is working against who you are" #FiresideChat

There is no better time than right now to embrace all God has designed you to be. He did not create us to remain in a posture of frustration and hurt, but He did call us to reflect on those things that make us uncomfortable so we can ultimately move to the next level and another dimension. The mask you've worn has been your attire far too long. Dreams you've put on your life's bookshelf never to be opened and discovered, pain you have carried and never sought opportunity to release, unhealthy relationships that seemingly have never entered a space of positivity, are ready for release; and the time for you to obtain your peace is NOW!

Over the years while growing up as a preacher's kid and grandson of a Pastor, I've witnessed that if you liberate yourself from what others think about you and emancipate yourself from the bondage of your past, you will soon begin to walk in the best days of your life. For you to move when everyone is static, the mentality must be developed whereas, "Who God is creating me to be, has nothing to do with who you say I used to be." #FiresideChat

I had the fortunate opportunity to serve my country in the United States Navy. While I'm humbled by the experience, my career was not as decorated as some of my shipmates. Over the years, I beat myself up internally because I had every opportunity to shine and mirror my father's naval career in that he retired. However, I had to go through some very tough days so I can experience my best days. The obvious point is, do not become so engulfed with the "why" that you lose sight of "how."

- Look "how" God brought me through
- Look "how" God carried me through
- Look "how" God protected me

The "why" component is sometimes a trap of the enemy to keep you focused on your situation and not the Savior. The "why" will keep you in a state of concern versus centering your thoughts on the comforting arms of God. To move forward, you have to shift your thoughts and shift your focus, then in return, God will shift your life for the better. Arguably, my favorite is the "how" factor. After your thoughts have shifted, you can begin to witness to the song, "I don't know how he is going to do it, and he didn't say when, but I know God will make a way." How wonderful is that? We are not responsible for the "how," but we have a powerful God who is solution oriented enough to take us from broke to better, burdened to blessed, apprehensive to anointed and bitter to better. To move forward after facing adversity will require a type of faith that will bring you completely outside of the status quo and normalcy. In fact, this level of faith will have others looking at you with a "side-eye." But don't concern yourself with how you look rather, what God is doing in your life. I love the story of Abraham and Isaac in Genesis 22. It embodies and symbolizes the level of faith we should have if we are to march and move forward. God gave specific instructions to Abraham to pick up everything and go to the land of Moriah; and at that place, he would kill his son. The interesting concept is that God did not withhold information from Abraham. He knew what his assignment was as he was traveling, yet he continued to sojourn until he reached Mount Moriah. The exceptional thing about Mount Moriah was that it was place Abraham had never been before. It was unfamiliar territory. The terrain had not been traveled too often, yet Abraham's FAITH compelled him enough to do what the Divine instructed him to do. Abraham had every opportunity to turn around, back out, and even question this assignment. I believe Abraham realized for him and his family to be blessed, he had to see beyond the burden of the moment because the bigger picture produces the greater reward; thus, he chose reward over relief. If we choose relief, we cannot experience the totality of what God has designed for us. Therefore, it is incumbent for us to follow God's direction in faith. Of course, relief will make you feel better because you want out, but it will not produce a divine outcome.

This level of faith that you need to possess when moving forward after adversity is called "Audacious Faith."

Audacious is defined as showing a willingness to take surprisingly bold risks.

When you think of someone embodying the characteristic of audaciousness, I want you to take on a mind frame of fearlessness, courageous, and in some cases heroic. Audacious faith is the ability to move forward in faith when you know exactly what you face, but knowing you have someone who supersedes you. This concept of audacious faith will catapult you into a space where God will give you strength, resolve, and fortitude beyond your human capacity and that is called "anointing." God will anoint you when you trust him and operate with audacious faith.

"God cannot release abundance if you possess apprehension." #FiresideChat

The anointing God graces you with is attached to your assignment. You are endowed with anointing for the express purposes of action. If you intend on not acting, then God cannot expand your territory. Your anointing is packaged with power, purposed with plans, and God will provide the provisions.

When I move, there is an expectation for God to move. When He moves, breakthroughs happen, blessings are released, deliverance is experienced, healing is evident, and before you know it; time has passed with you "MOVING FORWARD," even after adversity.

If it is your heartfelt desire is for God to unlock your best days, the key is for YOU not to be addicted to your own comfort. Comfort and audaciousness are not synonymous because God's intentions are to stretch you beyond your comfort so the end result is someone actively producing what was already inside of them.

Chapter 3

What's Your Equation?

We've all gone through various levels of school whether high school, undergraduate or post graduate level education. We all have taken some form of math during our academic experiences. For me, any type of math was my nemesis possibly because I had to work harder than others did or simply the equations were an inescapable agent I was not willing to overcome. Nonetheless, we use math daily to count money, utilization of Microsoft Excel, or counting your "ducks" to pay your bills, equations are the inescapable agent as I mentioned. Take this for a thought, if we use equations daily, and in some cases using them subconsciously, could we not develop an equation to assist us in Unlocking Our Better Days? Absolutely! This equation will not only accelerate your "Moving Forward" phase, but if you utilize this equation enough it will guide you even in the darkest of times.

This equation is not convoluted or complex but will require all three components. Excluding any of them will only cause setback versus experiencing the comeback.

Attitude + Aptitude = Altitude. I can only imagine your immediate thoughts as you solved life's most persistent question after enduring pain, where do I go from here? The answer is of course in the title of the book (FORWARD), but for us to have the most effective understanding the line of delineation must be given.

Let's start with **ATTITUDE**! When I was growing up, my beautiful mother, Cheryl Chatman, consistently said to the point that it became redundant, "Attitude is everything." I never completely took grasp of the statement until I experienced the most challenging times of my life and realized if your attitude is poisoned by pessimism, the probability of you moving forward is not promising. Very easily, any of the other "A's" in the equation could have gone first. I'm sure an effort would have been made to make it fit and sound extra pretty, but it would not have fit because attitude comes first. Attitude is everything. Your happiness during critical times is contingent on your attitude. Having a positive attitude somehow triggers something in your brain to keep pushing, keep fighting even when you don't feel like it. Will you still feel injured while experiencing pain and trying to manage your attitude? Yes Indeed! BUT your attitude is the launching pad for you to unlock your better days. Injuries are not indicative of God's involvement, meaning yes you were injured or hurt, but God in Heaven knows and requires us to maintain optimism and faith then he will take care of the rest.

On countless occasions, I've witnessed the most gifted, talented, and skillful individuals utterly fall because of their attitude. As the cliché says, it will either make you or break you. Attitude is the driving mechanism to draw you into a space only you and God can enter and be intimate. Think of it from this perspective, God's son endured everything beyond comprehension. Do you think God wants to hear constant gripping about our struggles? Sure, He has an attentive ear, but our deliverance is contingent on our attitude. Growing up as a "Pastor's Kid," I've seen the misfortune of individuals being overcome by what they are going through. On the other hand, I've witnessed cancer patients persevere even after the prognosis was not favorable. Vividly, I recall working at a nursing home in Orlando, Florida, as a Rehab Technician. My responsibility was to transport all therapy residents to our gym for a series of exercises. The patients' medical conditions varied from massive strokes, heart attacks, car accidents resulting in paralysis, and progressive cancer. In all of my two years working there, I did not ever experience anyone with a poor attitude because of their condition. That job taught me so much about attitude and how powerful it can be to encourage others in the midst of them facing adversity.

May I give you a practical example? When I was 3 ½ years old, my mother was diagnosed with multiple sclerosis that took her 20/20 vision. To this day, her sight has never returned. Of course, at that tender age, I did not know what was going on or understand the magnitude of the circumstance. All I knew was, mommy could not read to me anymore, mommy could not drive me to the candy store, and mommy was extremely fatigued. Imagine having to embrace a new sense of normalcy, but still maintaining a household, raising two young children and being a U.S. Navy wife, while taking care of SELF. My fearless mom accepted the challenge and decided that while she had multiple sclerosis, MS did not have her. My mom picked herself, up accepted her "new normal," and made the best of what was delivered to the front step of her life. In all of my 32 years of living, I have NEVER heard my mom complain about her vision loss or her diagnosis. She is the truest epitome of a positive attitude in spite of her surroundings. She wrote a book, received countless awards, and made endless television appearances. The true definition of a survivor is one who embraces their new normal and moves forward with a sense of understanding that this is not the end.

Now that you have a keen understanding of the first "A" of our inspirational equation, let's dive into the second component, **APTITUDE.** Aptitude is the natural ability to do something to which we possess by God's grace. If we parallel that to our lives and the experiences we have to inevitably overcome, I would emphatically let you know there is something inside of you that can overcome the biggest challenges. The elephant in the room is the question you are asking me. If I have something in me naturally, then why I am still not able to move forward? Your answer lies in your inability to purify your attitude in spite of your experience or challenges. If you are reading this book, then you indeed are BLESSED. The mark of a true survivor is the person who maintained a positive attitude regardless of their pressures. They realized the PROMISE is greater than their PAIN. The ultimate survivor will **BE**come everything that God has designed them to be. So often we focus on everything wrong and we under value what is right. (That was good!) Shift your gears to your deliverance versus attending to your dilemma and you will see the miraculous hand of God smoothing out your path just so you can experience unspeakable peace. Sure the road to fulfilling your divine assignment will be encountered with the most difficult experiences that seemingly will take the life out of you, but you are the determinant that will either stand of sulk. Moving Forward is a process and just like many sporting teams who took this phrase by storm to motivate their team "trust the process" so should we. I've witnessed colleagues, supervisors, and Pastors, box aptitude to a corner of physical ability, athletic talent, or a particular skillset, which is well within the definition. However, if we are going to be overcomers, then we must believe there is something inside of us beyond our human capacity that God has strategically birthed in us to persevere and conquer the roughest days. While God gave us the aptitude or natural ability to overcome so we can BEcome, He has also given us authority over the enemy. Isn't that amazing? We have the aptitude and authority over our struggles, over the enemy, over the difficulties of life, and we will not even have to ask God for this power because He's already supplied it to us. The Bible says in Luke 10:19, "I have given you authority (aptitude) to trample on snakes and scorpions and to overcome the power of the enemy and nothing will injure you." That is tremendous news to know. God thought so much about you and me, He gave us the necessary resources for sustainability even though he was experiencing pain and suffering himself.

    Over the course of my career in healthcare, I've learned so many things that helped me grow significantly. When I take a 180-degree look back and recall the roller coaster moments and emotions, realization sets in that I had what I needed all along but underestimated the power that was already within me.

Affirmation Activity - Repeat until you cross the threshold of assurance.

"I'M BUILT"

"I'M POWERFUL"

"I'M FIERCE"

"I'M STRONG"

"I'M DETERMINED"

"I'M TOUGH"

Don't you feel empowered? The purpose of our affirmational activities is obvious, which is "Life and death is in the power of the tongue" Proverbs 18:21. The other ideology is when you speak, you believe; when you believe, you change how you think. My intent is to help you change how you think or help you shift your vantage point from the vicissitudes of life to your VICTORY. If God declared we have the aptitude to move forward, then that should immediately change how we view the tornadic moments in our lives. When you are saddled in the midst of life's most inclement situations, you have the authority for it to cripple you or it to become motivation. It becomes problematic when your inspirational equation does not either have Attitude or Aptitude. You have to come to a place where the decision is made that you are in control. Because of that, the enemy can bring its best shot. The fight may last more than 12 rounds, and you may come out with bumps, bruises, and maybe some cuts, but just like boxing, you must have a great corner man to be victorious and ours is JESUS! Injuries are NOT indicative of God's Involvement because HE is always protecting you from malicious attacks and HE is always a great representation of compassion when we need it the most.

Altitude is the last component of our inspirational equation and is the climax or end result to a series of demonstrative acts of resolve and perseverance. Everyone, unfortunately, will not reach their highest altitude all because of their attitude. For your destined altitude to be reached, it comes with a price, but what doesn't? It will cost you tears, pain, and suffering, but never concern yourself with the end result that you lost sight of what it takes for you to rise. Everyone wants to experience the lights of success or the peaceful natured feeling of knowing your labor was not in vain. It is in those tornadic moments that we grow a deeper appreciation for the sovereignty of God.

Chapter 4

Managing Your Moments

How many times have you read articles about managing your finances, managing your time, or managing your anger? Has it ever clicked that if you're doing all of that managing shouldn't you know how to manage your moments? The truth is, we all will have our "moments," but the person who will experience the unlocking of their better days is the one who has/will manage their moment(s) most effectively. In this chapter, I want to provide you with tips and tools to manage life's most miserable moments and it could be as easy as ABC.

Did you know that after reading the first paragraph of this book you have already achieved a milestone in managing your moments? As I said earlier, "Truth is, we all will have our moments," and that is the acknowledgment phase. Acknowledging you are having a moment is the direct path to managing your moments effectively. I am not a physician or psychologist, but it lends itself back to my example of falling off the bike and being able to identify and assess the situation then working towards the resolution. If an alcoholic never acknowledges the issue he or she will not be able to fundamentally live in sobriety. Many times there is a certain level of denial that takes place which will prevent you from effective management of your moments.

Today I encourage you to let go or release this notion that having a "moment" is a sign of weakness, deficiency, or instability, but more so the primer before God paints your beautiful narrative.

Acknowledging your hurt and pain is the acceptable time to cry, express remorse or sadness, but never allow those emotions to become the definition of your identity. It would be completely unfair to suggest we will never have moments or the opposite that it's unhealthy to have a moment. Rather it's therapeutic in that once your "moment of emotions" has been exhausted, there is a sense of emptiness for God to fill you with His Spirit and presence. Where the line needs to delineated is when your moment follows you into relationships, your marriage, and how you interact with others. If you ever expect to move forward from adversity or challenges, then you will need to make a decision whether this will become who you are. Moments should always be temporary. I remember growing up as a young boy in Jacksonville, Florida. While sitting on the porch listening to stories from my great-grandfather and great-grandmother, Herbert and Letha Nicholson, who would give me nuggets. One of the most memorable nuggets was, "You may be down, but don't stay down. Give yourself 24 hours to cry, scratch or weep, but once the 25th hour comes, pull yourself up."

Minimizing what you are going through is never my intent, but the specificity of this chapter is to serve as a reminder to you that YOU can move forward, you can push through even in the face of hurt and pain.

Now that we know that acknowledgement is a key component in managing our moments, the second piece to our ABC concept is "Break-Away." If you are to move to a space of strength, then you will need to break away from certain people, which may include family, friends, colleagues, roommates, neighbors, or whoever is becoming detrimental to you as a person. When you are going through your moments, the very last thing you need is someone to set you back because they don't have the capacity to provide you what you need to continue on the road of healing. Anyone who knows me well, knows I love sports and possibly one of my favorites is NASCAR. Sports racing can teach us so much about life, if you pay close enough attention to the things that are going on simultaneously. Imagine five drivers on the last lap of an intense 500-mile race. Each of them are fighting for a place in the winner's circle, until a car comes out of nowhere breaking away from a group fighting for 2nd, 3rd, and 4th place. This driver is now the winner of the race and proceeds to the winner's circle in joy and happiness because he or she did not allow the surroundings to control the remainder of the race. I know you are thinking how and what does that have anything to do with me managing my moments. The answer is, it has everything to do with it. If you are going to come to a space of victory, in spite of what you've been through and being in the back of the pack, then it's incumbent upon you to break yourself away from people.

- Be careful who you decide to pour your Pain to.

The reason it's critical to break away from certain individuals is that you cannot afford to share something in confidence with someone who in turn breaches the confidentiality you thought existed. Not only are you on your journey of moving forward and unlocking your better days, but now you have to deal with someone who has compromised the trust you gave them. The lesson is, not everyone should be privy to knowing what you're going through even if it's public. When you are trying your best to manage your moments, your favorite word should be "removal."

- Removal from toxic energy
- Removal from toxic people
- Removal from toxic environments
- Removal from toxic relationships

Breaking away has little to do with the other person, but has all to do with you. Your position and posture is of healing, not continued hurt. The second component of breaking away is in another #FiresideChat.

- Become Intimate with an Intercessor

When you are managing your moments, find a prayer partner who can intercede or go to God on your behalf without you ever asking them to do so. Find your partner without hesitation. There is a sense of urgency to speak to God so heaven can be shaken for you to gain healing and deliverance. The characteristic of this person should be consistently summed up in the word "hesitation." If you feel there is the slightest reservation, then this perceived intercessor may not be the right person for what you need in this particular season of your life. Please do yourself a favor and do not choose a family member out of default due to the dynamics of your relationship. Carefully examine the sincere intent of the person you choose. Generally you can go with your gut. After-all, God did give us the spirit of discernment.

    The last and possibly the most critical of the "ABC" methodology is being conscientious. During the times when you are best managing your moments, there needs to be a certain level of consciousness of your surroundings and the people who have influence over your life. I value this last component wholeheartedly because experientially I've witnessed that you have to be so conscious of what you allow to enter your ears because it will soon enter your heart. If the wrong thing enters your heart, it could be fatal in the figurative.

Managing your moments during this journey we call life is easy as ABC especially when we acknowledge our problems, break away from certain people and be conscientious of your surroundings. Assurance is found in the problem solver. When the moment becomes miserable over manageable, then you should take steps to for a period of reassessment. What needs to be reassessed? It could be an accumulation of things such as people, your environment, to give you a starting point. You must believe the problem solver can transfer your miserable moments into workable solutions and strategies. Your pursuit to finding the peace that passes all understanding needs to come from a place within your soul that suggests despite my reality, the facts suggest otherwise. When you compare fact versus reality, I'm confident facts will outweigh the latter.

Reality

- I lost a loved one and it is painful even after considerable time has passed.

- I lost my job: My savings and 401K have been depleted.
- My marriage has ended in divorce.

Facts

- He heals the brokenhearted and binds up their wounds. (Psalm 147:3)
- When you pass through the waters, I will be with you. (Isaiah 43:2)
- Keep him in perfect peace whose mind is stayed on you, because he trusts in you. (Isaiah 26:3)

Although the reality is uncomfortable and the moments you experience are turbulent, there is one thing about facts you cannot ignore in that it will fit you for troubled times. I can almost imagine what you're thinking even as you read. "All of this is easier said than done" and in some cases, you have a valid point, but transparently it will get frustrating at times. It will become confusing and in the midst of it all, it will be convoluted. There has to be an inner resolve to FIGHT!

- ❖ Depression
- ❖ Anxiety
- ❖ Divorce
- ❖ Pettiness
- ❖ Death
- ❖ Financial Ruin
- ❖ Loss of a job

While you are fighting you have to believe your PEACE is connected to what you RELEASE. What you are releasing does not suggest the pain no longer resides, but it no longer relegates your daily functionality.

Chapter 5

Divine Isolation

Over the years working in corporate America there has been a concept and phrase used consistently enough to drive the common person crazy and that is silo mentality. What is a silo mentality? Think of a silo as you standing in the middle of a n empty farm alone. Having that mentality in the business world causes departments within the company to stand alone and only being concerned with their projects or areas of concern. It has been said that silos within the company reduce employee morale and possibly contribute to the overall failure of a company or its products and culture. Silos are not healthy for growth and maturation and that leads us to the title of this chapter, divine isolation.

What's the difference between the two? When you are making your best effort to move forward after adversity, silos will eventually be the demise to your forward progression because essentially you are shutting out the others and completely not allowing the anointing to direct. Silos are detrimental and I've witnessed them to be destructive. Silos in this sense are intentionally designed to cause chaos and disorder, which results in confusion thus productivity will never be experienced. Let's be honest for a moment and realize you will never be able to go through life, any obstacle, any hurt, any pain, and any burden without the help of somebody. One of the most famous recognizable rhythm and blues songs of our time is "Everybody Needs Somebody," by the Blues Brothers. Never intentionally isolate yourself from others because you want to keep people away from circumstance versus receiving Godly counseling.

Granted, in your defense, you cannot involve or employ everyone to be the "go to" person in your time of need. But, be very careful that you are not shutting out the person who will walk with you, hold your hand, and carry you through to your best days.

Divine isolation is not a common phenomenon and is not an easily googled concept you can pull together for understanding and clarity. This ideology of divine isolation extends from a period in my life, July 2012 through December 2013, where God's power worked on me constantly. During this particular timeframe, I experienced despair, divorce, discouragement, doubt, discontentment, distress, depression, dejection, and despondency. For God to unlock my better days and for me to move to forward after adversity, HE had to intentionally and divinely isolate me from everything and everybody. During this time, I could not understand the reasoning or purpose, but in hindsight, it was for me to experience better days. God sometimes needs to isolate us from people and things to get our attention and that is called divine isolation. When people are not connected in the Spirit, divine isolation is oftentimes confused with antisocialism, or in some cases "goody too shoes." Quite frankly, it's neither of the two. It is God doing a perfect work in your life for you to get closer to experiencing the best days of your life after experiencing the worst. During my period of divine isolation, friends dropped off and family members who I thought were in my corner to encourage me were no longer accessible. Sure enough when God isolates He will provide the necessary resources for your new season. Until I knew wholeheartedly what God was doing (which was not until my heart was softened), I took issue to this concept of divine isolation. I posed these questions to God, and I'm sure you have done so while reading this chapter.

1) Why are you isolating me from people who have been good to me?
2) Why are you isolating me from things that give me satisfaction and gratification?
3) Why are you isolating me from things that provide me joy and happiness?

The answers to those questions were on the weather channel. Yes, I know your immediate thought is that it sounds strange—the weather channel. Yes ma'am and yes sir! When the seasons change to either summer, spring, winter or fall, there is an expectation that comes with each season for example:

Summer = Heat.

Fall = Mild temperatures and leaves changing colors

Spring = Subtropical and tropical climates

Winter = Polar and temperate climates

To the average reader you may have expressed gratitude for the quick meteorological explanation. However, to those who have been divinely isolated and cannot understand why, it's because each season of your life will require varying elements to witness the full glory of God.

To experience SUCCESS, God may need to SEPARATE you not from demonic people, but from people who have been good to you, but their season of help has expired.

To experience your REWARD, God may need to REMOVE toxicity from your life that would have derailed His purpose for you.

God works just like the seasonal changes. He provides us what we need in the particular season of our lives. For summer to be considered summer there needs to be the heat element. For winter to be considered winter the element is either snow or very cold temperatures. For spring to be considered spring the element is rain, mild temperatures, or pretty flowers (that was for my granny). For fall to be considered fall, leaves need to change colors and fall.

Think of it in this capacity, would it be considered summer if you are experiencing 25 degree weather, wind chills in the lower to mid-teens, and the expectation of 2-5 inches of snow? Absolutely not!

I will give it another shot. Would it be considered winter if temperatures were blazing in the mid to upper 90's with a heat index in the 105 degree range? Absolutely not!

Consequently, I know the reason for "divine isolation" is that whatever season God is preparing us for, the elements must be right and when they are, blessings are unexpected, and deliverance is exceptional. During this period I learned an incredible amount of things about who I was to my very core which would eventually allow me to communicate that in my service to others, committed relationships, and even in the workplace environment. There is power in divine isolation that you will find as a necessary thing for what God will do in your life.

So often we have allowed the need to be surrounded by the masses or the need to have an entourage and that will stifle the hand of God as he divinely isolates you. Entourages are not there to encourage and elevate, but to position you to relapse into depression and anxiety. How often have your experienced or witnessed when someone is "going through it" and their friends, crew or in this case entourage, persuades them to step out for the night and get their mind off things, let your hair down or in our modern day vernacular "TURN UP." I'm sure you are shaking your head in agreement that you have witnessed or experienced this because we all have been there. I'm not suggesting there will be moments when the need to enjoy dinner and a movie or a good comedy show is present and beneficial, but be leery this does not become your identity whereas it becomes a means to mask your pain.

    During my period of divine isolation, God strategically placed people in my life when and where I needed them the most. I never once questioned the authenticity of our friendships, genuineness, or sincerity of their hearts. It's the exact thing needed to push you through to unlock your better days and move forward after adversity.

There is a what, when, and where component I want you to keep a watchful and vigilant eye for as God begins to operate in the miraculous for your life.

God's power is so amazing and great that sometimes it is hard to digest how awesome His love for humanity is. This power I am referencing extends to the deepest part of your soul so much that WHATever you need to unlock your better days HE WILL PROVIDE. Now that differs from person to person, but omniscience of God will meet you in the very area of your need.

"When" is never in our control because it's always God's timing. HIS timing is something we will never be able to comprehend, but we are assured His timing is precise and perfect. Galatians 4:4 gives us the example that resonates to the core of Christianity. "When the set time had fully come, God sent his Son, made of a woman, made under the law." The loving nature of God is so evident in his decision to send his Son when he did. It was not a pleasant time in which to be born, especially for the one who would be the Messiah. People worshipped idols, sacrificed children, used religion to exclude and persecute. Yet in His perfect time, He saved them all and us too. Think of this, the very ones who would hang his Son on a cross were the ones He had sent His Son to save. Parallel that scripture to our "when" concept and it will concrete the notion that God's timing is perfect and whatever you need He will send it just in the nick of time.

Historically, the where factor is something that has not always been embraced or possibly misunderstood only because of one word: Receptiveness.

The hearts of men and women have not been receptive to the idea that God can use anybody to give you the word you need to move you forward to unlocking your better days. The "where" is not necessarily a location (some cases it be), but I'm referencing the "where" as to your heart. Is your heart sealed shut to the idea that God can bring your needs packaged in something unpleasant, but the end result is extraordinaire? Is your heart open or receptive to God bringing your keys to unlock your better days from someone who you least expect it from?

Never get so consumed with the "HOW God is" over the "HE WILL do it." I've grown to learn and appreciate the power of counsel and connection even after experiencing the challenges life presented. After going through a divorce and moving into a state of depression, my keys came in the form of three individuals who helped shape and transform me. Little did I know our connection would evolve into friendships far beyond what I could ever imagine. Dan Dugger, Sean McKinney, and Lionel (Big Bro) Campbell, I thank you for being there when and where I needed you the most, but also providing what I needed in the most critical time.

During the time Jesus walked this earth, He kept three men close who were Peter, James, and John. I believe Dan, Sean, and Lionel were my Peter, James, and John. God will do the same for you only if your heart is receptive to those whom God sends in your life.

Chapter 6

Responsibility and Ownership

One of my favorite words is responsibility. I oftentimes use it when mentoring our next generation because it is an increasingly loss concept. We live in a world that examples or suggests the easy thing to do is place blame on your neighbor. The comfortable thing to do is allow the fellow man to become the voice over your life without you ever taking ownership. Over the years, I have studied prisoners who were convicted of a crime. Although knowingly they committed this particular crime, which resulted in a prison sentence yet they maintain their innocence. It has always boggled my mind as to why a person would continue to maintain innocence when in their heart of hearts they know they are completely guilty. The conclusion is people lack taking responsibility and ownership for things that can impact their life, reputation, character or perception. I'm almost sure it sounds kind of strange that a prisoner serving time for a particular crime, regardless of severity, wants to keep in tack their perception that others may have of them, but it's true.

    The purpose of this chapter is not to focus on the prison system, but to express the critical need for you to take ownership and responsibility for your happiness, peace, joy, and cloud nine experiences. The definition of ownership is the right of possessing something and the definition of responsibility is the ability to act independently and make decisions without authorizations. Let me be completely clear in that you have the right to be happy in spite of mistakes, you have the right to walk with joy in spite of past pain, and you have the right to experience blessedness in spite of tragedy. Not only do you have the right of possessing hope, expectancy, and delight, but you can act independently suggesting you do not need prior authorization from anyone for jubilation to become present in your life.

    I remember growing up at 10 years old preparing for my first sermon and my mom helping me to write points and draw up my outline. Granted, this was well over 20 years ago, but I can recall sitting at our kitchen table talking, discussing, writing, planning, preparing, and praying. You're possibly thinking either how have I remembered so vividly this day, or what was the significance of this particular sermon preparation away from others. My mother and I finalized my topic, which was "Where Is Your Faith" and we were finishing my last point. But before she gave me what to write, she whispered in my ear "When you become an adult, I want you to always remember this because it will carry you through. Man will disappoint, but God will appoint." How true is that? How many times have people disappointed you? How many times have you depended on someone, but only to be disappointed because they did not keep their word?

This falls in line with our chapter title because the same way you cannot depend on others, you should not expect them to be the authorizers for your happiness, peace, and joy. Only YOU are responsible for the happiness that will be adopted into your life. One of my favorite gospel songs is, "Encourage Yourself" by Donald Lawrence. The words are so critical to us unlocking our better days and being able to move forward after adversity.

"Sometimes you have to encourage yourself, sometimes you have to speak victory during the test, and no matter how your feel, speak the word and you will be healed. Speak over yourself in the Lord. Sometimes you have to speak the word over yourself, the pressure is all around, but God is a present help. The enemy created walls, but remember giants they do fall. Life can hurt you so until you feel there is nothing left, encourage yourself in the Lord."

The necessity of encouraging yourself, assuming responsibility, and taking ownership of your happiness and peace is paramount to you moving forward past adversity because it's a mind over matter eventuality.

"The muscles in your mind are stronger than the muscles in your body" #FiresideChat

The power that resonates in a made up mind is astonishing on so many levels. How often have you witnessed someone with a determined mind whether it's good or bad to posture themselves to accomplish their intended goal? I remember meeting my fiancé for the first time and desiring to see her and talk to her daily. My mind was made up from the beginning to achieve a relationship of what I had already envisioned in my mind (to which it happened). Envision yourself on the other side of your pain and imagine yourself operating in another dimension after experiencing some of your most hellish moments.

Wise Solomon said, "For as he thinks in his heart, so is he" (Proverbs 23:7). As the title of this chapter would suggest, it is your responsibility to think you will make it through. Ownership belongs to you that will say, "I'm a survivor."

There is absolute power in a made up mind because it sends off divine waves to an enemy that desires to sift you as wheat. (Luke 22:31). To the amateur or even professional body builder, your immediate mind has maxed out for one repetition on the bench press at 215 pounds, but due to a mind that has power and is made up, not only have you exceeded the repetitions, the weight has become a non-issue. Today is the perfect time for you to take complete ownership and responsibility for your happiness and ability to move forward after adversity. Quite honestly, the enemy is not after your marriage, your children, your job, your home, he wants your FAITH. The enemy has a very cunning way to deceive the children of God because he assumes if their faith is shattered then they couldn't possibly believe in a Savior. Little does this "fella" know that our faith is not going to waver nor falter because on the other side of our adversity is a dimension that is boundless. The key to unlocking your better days is knowing who holds the key, and the person who is reading this book is the owner. Through reading this chapter my sincere hope is that you never depend on anyone to satisfy your happiness and provide you internal peace because that is your responsibility.

Happiness is within reach and you experiencing joy is an arms-length away, but the responsibility is yours whether you want to take ownership of your happiness. Too often when it comes to internal peace, joy, and happiness there is a sense of dependency and unfortunately, you will become easily disappointed. For you to unlock the best days of your life and be able to move forward after adversity commit yourself to the following

- Identifying where your pain is so God can demonstrate his miraculous power in your life.
- Marching forward in spite of what has weighed you down.
- Affirming your attitude in that you can get through anything in spite of what reality says.
- Effectively managing your moments is easy as ABC
- Divine isolation is not alienation, but God separating you for the next season of your life.

- Prior authorization is not needed for you to experience joy and happiness because the responsibility is yours.

Chapter 7

Immunity From Interruptions

By now, I'm confident you have regained control over your life in some capacity and taken a stance against the attacks of the enemy, but I must be completely honest with you. While the tools and motivation have been given, and I pray you will soon adopt them if not already, you are not immune from the interruptions of life. In fact, they will come. Just look at how the enemy tempted Jesus in Matthew 4 where he tempted Him to turn stones into bread, take Him into the highest point of the temple, and also the mountain.

As you sojourn, remember the Spirit gives permission to the enemy to interrupt our focus. Can you only imagine Jesus after fasting 40 days and 40 nights how hungry He must have been? Instead of focusing His energy on healing others, Jesus is being tempted to turn a stone into bread. I believe the lesson is for us to not lose focus because we are then led astray and cannot fundamentally operate in our purpose. (Stay Focused.) Whatever you do, please do not allow a spirit that is beneath the Holy Spirt to disrupt your focus and get you off course.

The Spirit does give permission to disrupt our focus. My encouragement to you is not to give energy to the permission, but shift your mind to God's promises. It's so easy to centralize our thoughts on the permission, or begin questioning God as to who, what, when, where, and how. However, the Promises of God outweigh anything that could possibly go wrong in our lives. Always remember, the Promise is more important the Permission. The Permission is where God is going to prepare you, and the Promise means you have been equipped for the battle. (That was Good!)

Let's all be honest, the enemy is after your hope. Your hope is the blueprint; your faith is the building material. If the enemy interrupts your hope, he stops the project. Don't allow your hope to be hijacked only for the project not to be completed. The project God is building and bridging inside of you is massive and organically something the world has never seen before. We are depending on YOU; yes YOU, to see this thing through.

Granted, we all have faced various interruptions of life, and some have been bottled up in clichés.

- When it rain it pours – Interruption
- If it's one thing, it's another – Interruption

Whatever the interruption that comes knocking at your door, you should expect them because it's all in preparation for what is being constructed for you to change the world, for you to make a difference, and for you to change the course of someone's life for the better.

www.ingramcontent.com/pod-product-compliance
Lightning Source LLC
Chambersburg PA
CBHW072009090426
42734CB00033B/2324